The Death of a Wombat

The Death

# of a Wombat

IVAN SMITH

drawings by CLIFTON PUGH

Charles Scribner's Sons ■ New York

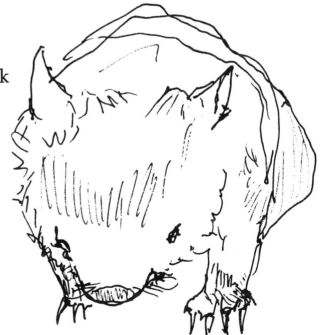

Foreword

H.R.H. The Duke of Edinburgh

Nature affects people in many different ways, and attitudes to nature can vary from total ignorance and indifference to total obsession. It is almost impossible for us to be objective about nature because we are part of it. We are animate while all our splendid creations, whether they are the products of artistic or engineering genius, are inanimate, dead, lifeless. We have more in common with any living creature than with the best of our more familiar mechanical companions, such as motor cars or television sets.

I rather suspect that it is this recognition of the relationship between men and animals which is at the bottom of the anthropomorphic attitude; the giving of human qualities to animals. Whatever may be the reason, there is a long history of extremely popular illustrated stories about humanized animals. They may not represent reality but they make a deep and lasting impression.

The Death of a Wombat is in this tradition and it is obviously a brilliant combination of artistic and literary talent. The result is a deeply moving document.

PRESIDENT, AUSTRALIAN CONSERVATION FOUNDATION

Introduction

My first meeting with the Australian wombat was a very
happy one. For me it was gratitude at first sight. It came about
by way of a postcard, which I happened to see on a rack in
my local news agency. I bought three copies, forgot what else
it was I had been wanting, and walked into a little park to
study every detail.

There was minimal information on the back of the card:
"Australian native animals. The wombat—a burrowing,
herbivorous, nocturnal marsupial." It was little to go on, but
I was sure he was what I had been looking for for weeks.

I had been wanting to write a sort of allegory on the human
condition as I had been seeing it as a young man. I wanted
to synthesize certain groups of human characteristics and to
set these groups in contrast in order to say something about
human success and failure. I couldn't find a form for it,
and so I couldn't even begin to write.

The postcard changed that.

The wombat seemed to be friendly, stupid, innocent,
slow—all characteristics that I was looking for in the main
figure. I read some books about him, hoping hard that he
didn't have one or two highly unpleasant aspects to his
character. He hadn't. He had courage, and a certain amount
of resourcefulness and doggedness. The only drawback was
that he was nocturnal, but that could easily be ignored.

I read biologies of other animals of the Australian outback
and found all I wanted:

 the kangaroo—strong, tough, but too stupid to win
  through in a calamity;

the koala—decent enough, but unimaginative and
  unenterprising, among the first types to go under in
  country-wide adversity;
the dingo—tough, resilient, and with the cunning that sees
  people through when times are out of joint;
the wombat—with the sort of gentleness and
  vulnerability that make nice guys finish last.

My reading led me to think that a bush fire would provide
a suitable social disaster common to the fates of these
animal symbols.

Like the great majority of Australians I have always been
a big-city dweller, and my knowledge of bush fires had been
confined to black-and-white newsfilm. Detailed descriptions
of them gave me a forcible impression of their ugly
ruthlessness. So thankfully, I was on my way; I could start
to write. In telling the story I have resorted to the word
"crump" to describe the wombat's shuffling motion;
this usage is my own invention.

The Death of a Wombat was written as a radio documentary
and has now been broadcast in several countries. I have
been very interested in individual reactions to it. An
American friend asked me if I saw something of the dingo
in President John F. Kennedy. An Englishman said he saw
something of the wombat in W. H. Auden. It might be better
not to mention some names that have been linked with the
kangaroo and the koala.

What is heartening to me these days is that, although
many people realize that the wombat has a hard time of it in
our society, and generally goes under in any social
turbulence, he nevertheless represents what is widely held
to be worthwhile, and even admirable.

The Death of a Wombat

It is night.

The moon is there.

The story begins in dry bushland,

bristling from the rough skin of Australia.

Not much thunder is heard in the inland

of Australia. Around the coastline it is heard,

when water, hugging the earth,

sends on its moon-drawn tides to crash against the land,

beating against the thrust-up arms of rock,

12

and the crushed-up foam of breakers races to the beaches like a horde of angry rats.

But in the inland there is not much thunder.
Sometimes there is the distant rumble of massed kangaroos in flight.
Sometimes there is the fierce night-dancing of forgotten men.
Almost always there is silence, and there is silence now,
and briefly the bland and stupefying moon
eases the land of the torment of the drought.
The days are dry and hard, and the animals suffer.

But now, for a few hours, snakes are loosely coiled,

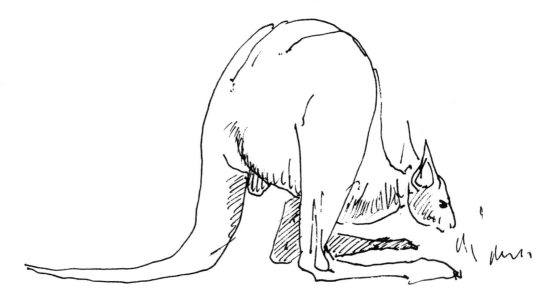

wombats sleep in their holes,

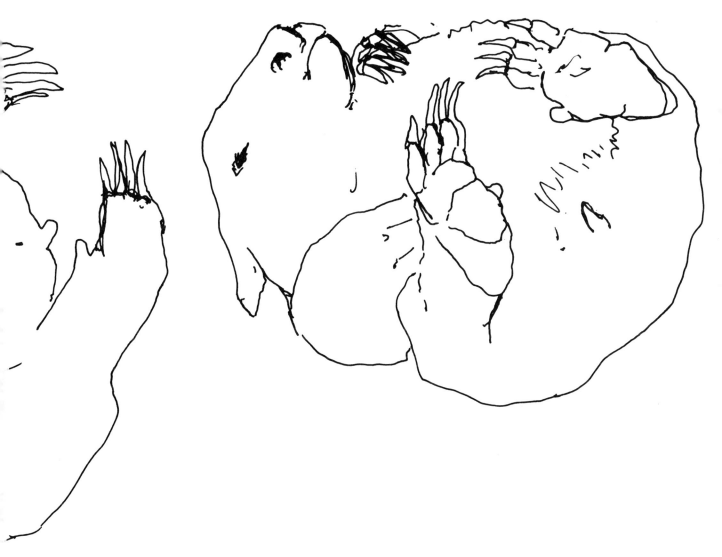

birds' beaks sag in the trees,
and the flies are still.

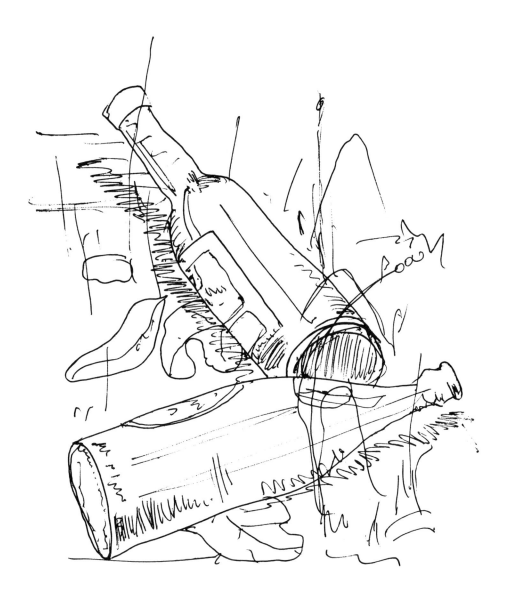

A road runs through this part of the country. Near it is the
quiet preparation for another sort of thunder. A bottle lies here,
brown, unbroken. Tomorrow it will bend thirty square inches
of summer sunlight into five. This will go on for some hours.
Before noon, more than twelve hundred square miles of bushland
will be totally destroyed.

But, for the time,
the flies sleep,
the birds are cool,

and the wombats are dozing heaps
in their holes.

Now the dawn . . .
the beginning again . . .
the Australian bush-dawn . . .
the quietest pageant of the earth!

The sun, not yet seen, begins to sketch designs of rock and hill.
A silver edging slowly marks out sacs and rims of cloud.

The tips of trees
begin the day's thinking
while their roots
still lie asleep.

The first bird calls are over.
The crest of a ridge grows sharp,
and the side in darkness for a time grows darker.
The air becomes warmer with every minute.
In a paddock sheep have waked and are standing,
moving slowly over the land as the foam of calm water
might move over rocks and sandbars.

Animals and birds are busy early. One of the busiest
is the wombat. He has to be busy because he's so slow
For him it takes the whole long day to get any
sort of work done. There is food to get,
and stones to dig, and a bit of the burrow to mend.
There are leaves to find for his tunnels
and things to visit.

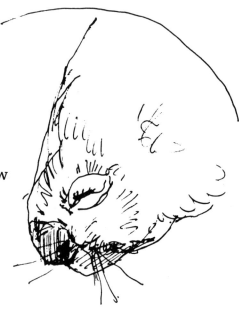

The wombat comes from a pleasant family, fussy and gentle,
slowminded and polite. He is a close relative of the koala bear,
who took to the trees a long time back to get away from it all.
The wombat has a short snub nose and short, stubbed legs
and a short-range mental life.
He is a ponderous plump of meat with a lurching walk.

Everything likes a waddler. The wombat lurches on,
slowly minding his own business. There are bits of bark to find
and things to visit. And everything likes a waddle and crump,
and slowly home to dinner on time, and a gentle doze
in a well-made hole, and early thoughtless yawns,
and waddle and crump again.

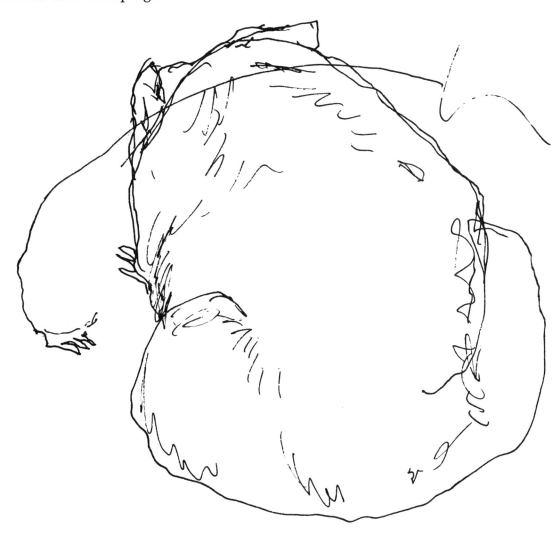

If an animal's walk could suggest any words,
for the wombat they might be these:
"I'm good morning to everything!
Isn't it nice familiar earth!
I'm waddling on and I like to crump.
I'm a ponderous plump of meat and that suits me.
I'm a waddler and slow, and I'm timid and stupid.
I waddle on,
and I waddle slow,
and even waddling nowhere, I still like waddling on."

It's good that the bush is kind to the wombat.

The trundling snout is pushed along by the high,
ungainly rump. From a wombat's-snout view, the world perhaps
seems strange. But nothing would want to hurt him.
The wombat has no enemy.

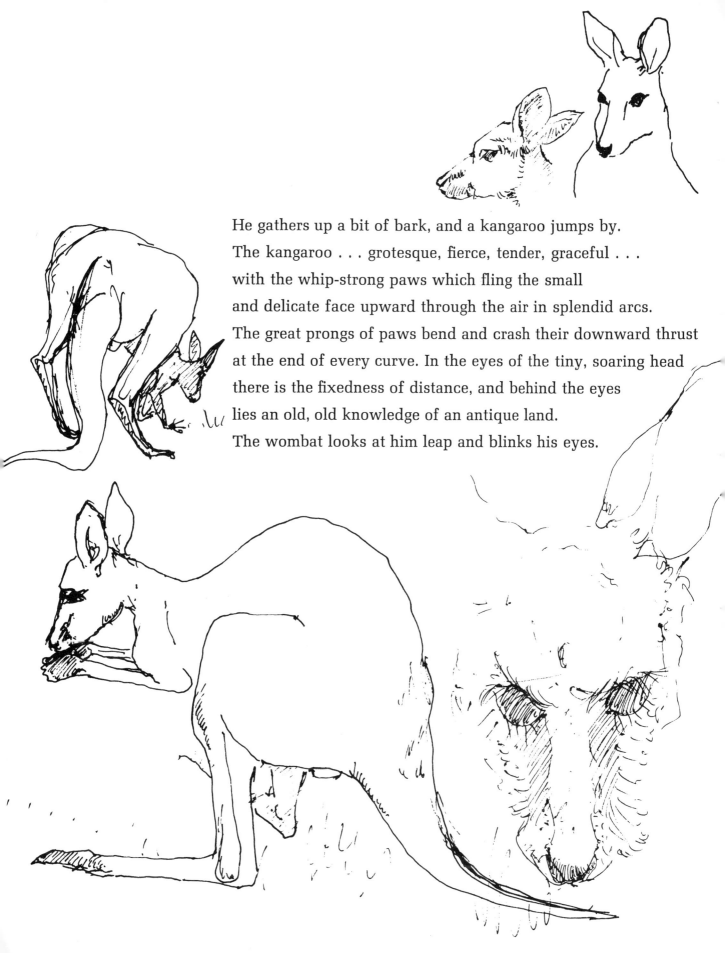

He gathers up a bit of bark, and a kangaroo jumps by.
The kangaroo . . . grotesque, fierce, tender, graceful . . .
with the whip-strong paws which fling the small
and delicate face upward through the air in splendid arcs.
The great prongs of paws bend and crash their downward thrust
at the end of every curve. In the eyes of the tiny, soaring head
there is the fixedness of distance, and behind the eyes
lies an old, old knowledge of an antique land.
The wombat looks at him leap and blinks his eyes.

The wombat almost stumbles over a brown, round thing of glass.
That's what comes of trying to think
and letting the waddle and crump take care of itself.

The big rump tumbles from side to side as he goes along to find more bark.
Unconcerned, the friend of all the bush moves away
from the prism of glass that will lead to the killing of almost
every living thing in the bush before twelve o'clock.

The sun pours onto the bottle near the road.

Half-past eight.

The curve of the glass
bends the light to a slim, searing line
across the dry leaves underneath.
The edges of the leaves begin to curl.

On the way back to his hole, the wombat hears a muttering
in the trees. He is waddling underneath koala cousin,
who sits and nibbles a gum tip on a branch.
Not many koalas left now, because drought has stifled the
gum tips that keep the koala alive.
There are many small bears
dead on the ground.
The wombat surely likes koalas,
furry and round, with flat,
painted noses,
as inoffensive
as himself.

Half-past nine.

The jagged leaf-edges blacken.
Steadily the sunlight curves to its scythe-edge,
one foot long.

At the edge of his hole, the wombat lurches over a brown
bush snake. The snake, knowing perhaps that the
wombat's eyesight is not very good, slithers himself away.
Everything likes a waddler.

Ten o'clock.

The base of the bottle cracks off
with a sharp, small explosion.
There is a brief flicker of flame.

The wombat trundles the sand away,
using his nose as a spade.
Then he lies on his side to dig
and mends his burrow.
He makes a much better job of it
than the impatient rabbit does.

Half-past ten.

A puddle of fire spreads around the bottle.
The glass shatters.

The wombat does not keep
any sort of lookout.
He has no enemies.
Only an inexperienced
dingo might attack him.

The wombat can hurt the dingo.
He backs into a fight,
and the dingo learns that teeth
have no effect on thick, fat-encrusted hide.
The wombat waits till the moment comes
to thrust his fat rump up and backward,
cracking the dingo's skull
against a log or a stump.

A quarter to eleven.

A flashing of a wagtail in the air.
The wombat grunts, and the wagtail carries off
his small beakful of fur. The wombat does not mind,
and he backs himself against his tunnel wall
to press the sand down.
Then he is off with waddle and crump
to find a stone.

The thunder has begun!

A eucalypt explodes
and there is the first temple of flame.
Flames spread through the undergrowth and send up blossoms
of fine ash. On a distant farm, cocks crow at midday.
The roaring startles rabbits,
and they scamper to their burrows.

The flames lash out at neighboring trees
like the tails of angry cats. A mushroom of muddy smoke
covers the sky. The sun is a far-off scarlet disk.
Scalding sap splinters bark casings.

A short, round thing of glass has wakened the terror
of the ages.

Eleven o'clock.

It is one long bellow of fire!

The snake that let the wombat go makes
hysterical whiplash patterns in the air
and hisses out his life.

The dingo, cunning and unconquerable,

unconquerable through his cunning,

turns to watch the screaming dance of the approaching fire.

The tutorship of his line of sires, and of his own experience,

crowds forward in his mind. The dingo is the knotting up of nature

into a cord of hard, unfraying toughness. He is savage.

He is resolution without concession. He is animal that masters.

He is ruthlessness, courage, and majesty.

The dingo stands. He pants easily now, and waits.

He saves his breath and his blood.

He alone has a chance to live. The long, old

knowledge of his line of sires moves into the strong,

spread paws and the heavy-muscled jaws.

He must race through the fire!

Others will race away from it, turn from it.
The wombat, cut off from his burrows, will try to reach
the only river left with water by the drought.
The koala cannot escape. He will, of course, fight for life
in the prison to which he has committed himself,
the trees that grow the only food that he can live by.
The kangaroo may have a better chance.
His huge legs might be faster than the fire.
Even if the wombat turned, went through the fire,
he still might be too slow, and the wombat is very slow.
But the dingo has a chance, and he lies down now
as the fire approaches, flops on his chest
and splays out his paws, and pants very easily
to save his heart. He closes his eyes and listens
to the flames. The marvelous fine mesh of muscle
at the root of either ear manipulates the pointed shapes
with delicate precision. In perhaps three minutes his contest will come.

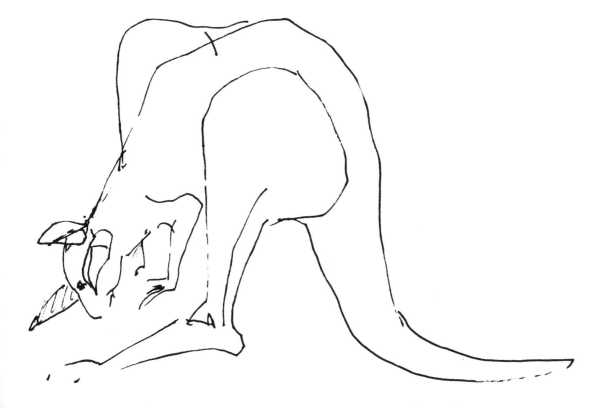

There is a waddle and half a crump.
The wombat stops and stares at a tree.
There is a sound in his ears that he has heard before.
Something is wrong. A dingo canters past
and he has his mouth shut. And where have the rabbits gone?
They are always flying in and around the bushes,
but not now. The kangaroos seem to be bounding to a gathering
somewhere behind him. The air has grown warmer
and he has heard this noise before.
Go back to the burrows. Crouching without a sound
in the burrows he has tunneled into the earth
is safety. But his burrows are there, where the noise is!
Noise . . . and the air getting hot . . .
and the animals gone!

The blaze has blackened eighty yards of land.
In the next hour it will burn out twenty miles.
It is not a fast fire yet . . .
twenty miles an hour, but it is too fast for many
of the beings of the bush. For the wombat,
half a mile in an hour, it is much too fast.

The wombat pushes up his head.
Smoke chokes his nostrils.
With waddle and crump he moves ten paces on.
Still there is smoke.
His short snub nose is damp as the smoke
strains out his tear ducts to protect his eyes.

The river is half a mile away, and his instincts tell him: there!
With waddle and crump and lurching on he begins to see it,
twisted through the shimmer of smoke and tears.
It is very much hotter now but the lurching cannot be faster.
The rump, so much higher than the trundling, weeping head, grows hot.
If his fat were not covered by hide it would flash into flame.
Nothing matters now but desperate crump and waddle,
and the river still ninety yards away.

The fire, a half mile behind,
the river ninety yards ahead
. . . no odds for a wombat.
He is not an animal to survive the bush
when it thunders this way. Dozens of his koala cousins
have died in the trees. They were not able to move, of course,
but they clung on hard to the branches as the skin was burned
like fresh, wet paint from their snouts—
gripped on hard till their hearts were stopped with smoke
and they fell like small, round torches,
lost in the flames.

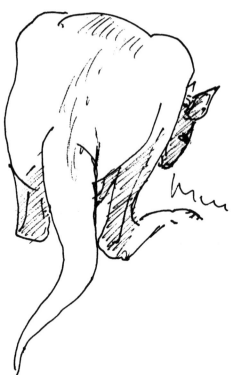

At first the kangaroo easily outpaced the fire. With a lope of forty miles
in an hour he has kept the flames well behind him.
The snakes and the koalas die; the dingoes wait their chance;
the kangaroo leaps on, and rests, and then takes up again
his ancient choreography of limbs and head.

The black smoke thickens in front of his face,
and the thunder behind the wombat blots out the noise
of the racing fires in the undergrowth.
These will reach him first . . . and destroy him.
The line of flame spans over thirteen miles,
a holocaust that knows nothing of the wombat.

The dingo moves himself to his feet

with the shouting flame two hundred yards away.

He shakes himself briefly like a dog

and then tilts back his head with the action of a wolf.

He starts forward, moving easily to meet the fire.

And as he moves, his body sinks lower

and the paws work harder on the ground

giving an athlete's rhythm . . . working harder . . .

and then the long, lean head sits low, the body gathers speed

with the powerful galloping action of the paws.

Seconds before he meets the flames, the dingo reaches cheetah-speed.

He plunges through them, eyes shut,

head thrust down between the flashing forward legs.

Over the whole land the sky is shut out.
Life is whipped from trees in the space of seconds.
An avalanche of burning sends the air into a frenzy.
Now to feed the thunder comes a wind,
and the twenty miles in an hour
are turned to seventy!

The flames have trapped the flying kangaroos.

They are tough and they leap with instinct.

Before they die they smell the sweet, strange scent of roasting flesh.

Their mighty paws still strike the ground while their heads loll downward
in death, jerking with each shudder of the body.

Then the crash, sudden and complete, no threshing on the ground,
with the tiny heads slewed back

. . . and the flames feed.

The river is yards ahead of the wombat's snout now,

just nine yards. Lurch and crump have sunk to slovenly heave and slide.

The flames have washed over him twice,

and there are little scrub fires in his fur.

The smoke has made him sob to catch his breath,

and the heavy, continual sobbing takes up most of his last strength.

His eyes are blind with hot fluid,

but his snout detects the river, six yards on.

His last fragments of life tell him: there!

The flames find him out again. He cries out in blind agony . . .

high squealing that doesn't match the lumpy body.

He slumps forward. The fire mounts over him.

His small shrieks are drowned by the noise.

And then, with a capricious change of wind,

the fire sweeps back. Soon it is half a mile away.

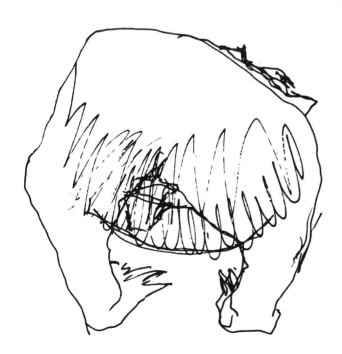

The wombat is left in the smoking bush,
undetectable black among black. Still breathing. Almost dead.
A travesty of wombat.
And yet, there is a lurch . . . waddling will not be possible again
and there is no strength left for crump . . .
and another lurch.
He makes the miracle
of reaching the river.
Slowly he slides
under water.

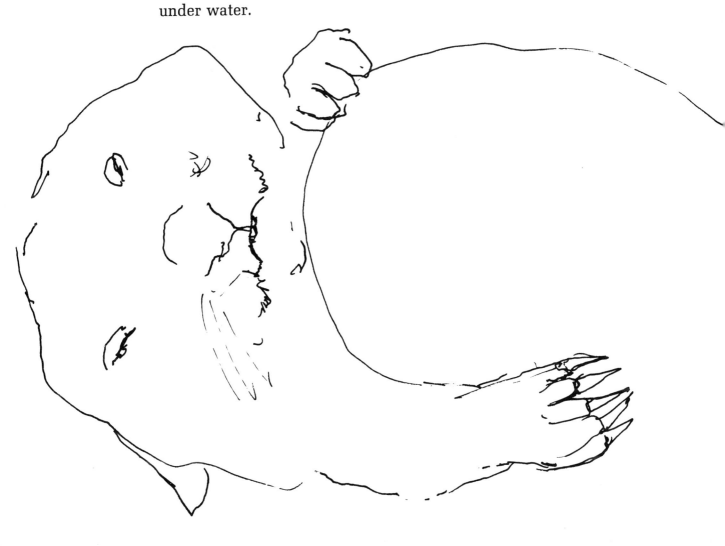

A mile away a dingo sleeps,
badly burned but living on.
Closer round, and much farther away,
there is death in the forms of shattered trees,
grotesquely twisted kangaroos,
goannas and koalas,
birds and rabbits and snakes.

Nothing moves, anywhere.

The wombat moves to a soft death now.

His fat, charred rump bobs slowly above the water as he drowns.

The last thing that he dimly knows is the gentle easing of his terrible burns.

A gesture perhaps, to the friend of all the bush,

to the meekness of waddle and crump?

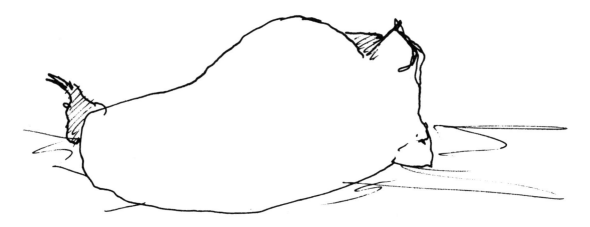

61

When the sun sets,
the thunder has gone.
The moon comes up.